THEY LOVE
FAMOUS BLACK QUOTATIONS.
AND YOU CAN QUOTE THEM.

"There is nothing like a timely, well-placed quote to make one's writing, speaking, or presentations sparkle. And to find that perfect quote there is no more convenient or easy-to-use source than FAMOUS BLACK QUOTATIONS. . . .Highly recommended."
> —*Black Collegian*

"FAMOUS BLACK QUOTATIONS will be useful for a different perspective in the classroom. And students will love its size and price."
> —**Edna Pruce, Associate Dean,**
> **Student Affairs, Northeastern University**

"Everywhere I go all over this country, African-American leaders are using FAMOUS BLACK QUOTATIONS."
> —**Jeremiah A. Wright, Jr., Pastor,**
> **Trinity United Church of Christ**

"Should have been issued years ago."
> —**Gwendolyn Brooks**

"Fantastic!"
> —**Julian Bond**

more . . .

"FAMOUS BLACK QUOTATIONS is so popular at our stores that it's hard to keep it in stock."

> —**Barbara Martin, manager, Shrine of the Black Madonna Cultural Centers and Bookstores, Detroit, Atlanta, Houston**

"I have been using my very first copy of FAMOUS BLACK QUOTATIONS since it came out in 1986. It is a wonderful collection and an extremely useful resource."

> —**Deborah Prothrow-Stith, M.D., Assistant Dean, Harvard School of Public Health, author of *Deadly Consequences***

"An invaluable reference. . . . The book provides a saying of substance for a variety of occasions. FAMOUS BLACK QUOTATIONS is truly a godsend."

> —**Judy Richardson, Blackside, Inc., education director and series associate producer, *Eyes on the Prize*, coproducer, *Malcolm X: Make It Plain***

FAMOUS BLACK QUOTATIONS

EDITED, SELECTED, AND COMPILED
BY JANET CHEATHAM BELL

1, 6, 12, 15, 17, 23, 24, 26, 27, 28, 29, 33, 37, 38, 42, 45, 46, 50, 51, 56, 58, 59, 60, 61, 64, 65, 67, 69, 71, 72, 73, 75, 76, 77, 80, 81, 82, 84, 85, 90, 91, 92, 94, 96, 101, 104, 109, 113, 115, 117, 118, 119, 120, 127,

WARNER BOOKS
A Time Warner Company

This Warner Books edition is published by arrangement with the author.

Warner Books, Inc., 1271 Avenue of the Americas, New York, NY 10020

Visit our Web site at http://warnerbooks.com

ⓦ   A Time Warner Company

Printed in the United States of America

First Printing: February 1995

10 9 8 7

Library of Congress Cataloging-in-Publication Data

Famous Black quotations / edited, selected, and compiled
    by Janet Cheatham Bell.
        p.   cm.
    Includes index.
    ISBN 0-446-67150-9
    1. Afro-American—Quotations. 2. Black—Quotations.
        I. Bell, Janet Cheatham.
PN6081.3.F36   1995
081'.08996073—dc20   94-33015
                                                  CIP

Book design by H. Roberts
Cover design by Julia Kushnirsky
Cover illustration by Synthia Saint James

To Kamau
who is always searching
for knowledge

Be skilled in speech so that you will
succeed. The tongue of a man is his sword
and effective speech is stronger than all
fighting.

> **The Husia**
> *sacred wisdom of ancient Egypt*
> *translated by Maulana Karenga*

In memory of my parents
Smith Henry and Annie Halyard Cheatham
who passed on to me all that they knew
from their ancestors, plus what they learned
on their own.
And of M. Earle Pitts who helped me when
I needed it most.

Comparisons of human genes worldwide
have produced a "family tree" of the human
race whose branches closely mirror the
branching of languages proposed by
linguists, leading to the startling suggestion
that all people—and perhaps all languages
—are descended from a tiny population that
lived in Africa some 200,000 years ago.

William F. Allman
U.S. News & World Report
November 5, 1990

Grateful acknowledgment is made to those who granted permission to reprint substantial excerpts from published works; and to people of African descent throughout the world and through the ages who continue to find strength in the Word and eloquently express themselves orally and in print.

The excerpt from the poem "Pebbles" from the book *Islands* by Edward Kamau Brathwaite, published by Oxford University Press, 1969, reprinted by permission of Oxford University Press.

The excerpts from "Song of Winnie" in the book *Winnie* by Gwendolyn Brooks, copyright © 1991 by Gwendolyn Brooks, published by Third World Press, reprinted by permission of the author.

Excerpts from the poems "Silver Cell" and "I Am A Black Woman" from the book *I Am A Black Woman* by Mari Evans, published by William Morrow & Co., Inc., 1970, reprinted by permission of the author.

The excerpt from the poem "Tune for Two Fingers" from the book *Nightstar* by Mari Evans, published by the Center for Afro-American Studies, University of California, Los Angeles, 1981, reprinted by permission of the author.

"Never Offer Your Heart to Someone Who Eats Hearts," from *Goodnight Willie Lee, I'll See You in the Morning* by Alice Walker. Copyright © 1978 by Alice Walker. Used by permission of Doubleday, a division of Bantam Doubleday Dell Publishing Group, Inc.

The excerpt from the section "Being Fitted," from the book *The Watermelon Dress* by Paulette Childress White published by Lotus Press, 1984, reprinted by permission of the publisher.

"Type"
Written by Vernon Reid
© 1990, Dare to Dream Music and Famous Music Corporation
Reprinted by permission. All rights reserved

ACKNOWLEDGMENTS

I am grateful to several people whose encouragement and assistance have been essential to my perseverance, but I received special support from my mom, Annie Cheatham, and from Mildred Morgan Ball, Julian Bond, John H. Evans, Alvin and Lydia Foster, Lee McCord, Edna Pruce, Vinita Moch Ricks, Madeline Scales-Taylor, Deborah and Charles Stith, Delores Logan Watson, and Arlene Williams.

Several people brought me quotations, many of which are included here. In that regard, I want to thank Laurie Wright, Judith Ball, Ron Watkins, and my son, W. Kamau Bell. I must also express my gratitude to Ursula McPike who kindly reads everything and gives me necessary feedback. Thanks as well to James, Reggie, Rosie, and Walter who consistently provide opportunities for me to grow.

CONTENTS

PREFACE

When did you last want a quotation by Du Bois, Booker T., or Douglass, but didn't know where to find one?

How long has it been since you wanted to use a particular quotation in a lively conversation, but couldn't recall the exact words, or remember who said it?

Have you ever been writing a presentation at home, in the office, or on a plane and wanted to conclude with a quotation, but couldn't think of the right one?

If you have ever been in any of these predicaments, this is the book for you. Of the many and varied quotations by persons of African descent, over four hundred of the best known, including several that will become better known, have been collected here for your benefit and enjoyment.

This collection of quotations was begun after many unsuccessful attempts to locate specific quotations by African-Americans that I wanted for one project or another. Since standard reference works either did not include any quotations by people of African descent, or included only a small fraction of what was available, I saved what I had found for future use. As my collection grew, I began to respond to specific requests from family and friends. The natural next step was to publish them so that they could be shared with others who might be similarly frustrated.

Verifying the quotations for publication has been a labor of love because it has required not only that I read the works of many masters of language, but also that I listen attentively when black people gathered to listen to a speech or to converse.

Both reading and listening reinforced what I had always known, that multifarious images abound in the languages we use. These images are both fecund and powerful whether the quotation is from the oral tradition of an indigenous African language, or written/spoken in one of the several European languages that people of African descent have made their own.

Moreover, the matters that concern us have remained consistent over the centuries from ancient Egypt to the present, though the inaccessibility of these words of wisdom has limited our familiarity with their earlier forms.

This collection is compact to maximize its handiness, but there are many, many more where these came from. Several of the quotations include the year in which they first appeared. That information is used when the date provides additional illumination for the quotation. Obviously, a collection of this size makes no claim to being either exhaustive or comprehensive, yet I have attempted to offer a range of thought, limited, of course, by my own human inability to read everything and be everywhere.

It is hoped that this small book represents a beginning of the collection and publication of quotations by people of African descent, and another indication of our respect for the potency of language.

—JCB

Struggle

✳ If there is no struggle, there is no
progress.

Frederick Douglass

There are few things in the world as dangerous as sleepwalkers.

Ralph Ellison

When you don't know when you have been spit on, it does not matter too much what else you think you know.

Ruth Shays

To name something is to wait for it in the place you think it will pass.

Amiri Baraka

The problem of the twentieth century is the problem of the color line.

W.E.B. Du Bois

As long as an educated and wealthy Nigerian can be "Jim Crowed" in Johannesburg on his own ancestral continent or can still see a Ku Klux Klan cross burning in Mississippi, or until Africans have their proportionate share of posts on the great corporations that control their economies, or until one sees black faces among the top elites throughout the Arab world and in Hispanic America and Brazil where they are more rare now than in the racist United States, mobilization *as blacks* is still necessary. . . . Worldwide black consciousness is a psychological reserve that can be mobilized to achieve local ends as well as to aid others as the liberation process continues on.

St. Clair Drake

I have a dream that my four little children will one day live in a nation where they will not be judged by the color of their skin, but by the content of their character.

Martin Luther King, Jr.

A community is democratic only when the humblest and weakest person can enjoy the highest civil, economic, and social rights that the biggest and most powerful possess.

A. Philip Randolph

In our particular society, it is the narrowed and narrowing view of life that often wins.

Alice Walker

When unacquainted with other modes of life than their own meet with the record of such actions, unless they are restrained by authority, they look upon them as sins, and do not consider that their own customs either in regard to marriage or feasts or dress or the other necessities and adornments of human life, appear sinful to the people of other nations and other times.

Saint Augustine

Would America have been America without her Negro people?

W.E.B. Du Bois

There are no good times to be black in America, but some times are worse than others.

David Bradley

Since so many black folk pray only
when troubled, God gets them in trouble
at least once a day.

Johnny Ray Youngblood

As legal slavery passed, we entered into
a permanent period of unemployment
and underemployment from which we
have yet to emerge.

Julian Bond

There is a debt to the Negro people
which America can never repay. At least
then, they must make amends.

Sojourner Truth

I have great fear for the moral will of
Americans if it takes more than a week
to achieve the results.

Michael S. Harper

The cost of liberty is less than the price
of repression.

W.E.B. Du Bois

Divestment is the one strategy that could bring about change with a minimum of violence. . . . The Sullivan Principles have made our chains more comfortable. What we want are the chains removed.

Bishop Desmond Tutu

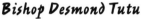

While I am in favor of universal suffrage, yet I know that the colored man needs something more than a vote in his hand. . . . A man landless, ignorant, and poor may use the vote against his interests; but with intelligence and land he holds in his hand the basis of power and elements of strength.

Frances Ellen Watkins Harper

I cannot accept the definition of collective good as articulated by a privileged minority in society, especially when that minority is in power.

Wole Soyinka

Here, equal justice under the law is prescribed only for the corporate rich and powerful. There are literally thousands of people imprisoned solely because of their race and poverty.

Benjamin F. Chavis, Jr., 1978

It is an historical fact that whenever the oppressor is called upon to define an indigenous product of the oppressed that product loses its functional value.

James G. Spady

It grew on me that we, black men especially, were expected to be subservient even in groups where ostensibly everyone was equal.

Shirley Chisholm

We wear the mask that grins and lies.
Paul Laurence Dunbar

No person is your friend who
demands your silence, or denies your
right to grow.

Alice Walker

Injustice anywhere is a threat to
justice everywhere.

Martin Luther King, Jr.

I'm sick and tired of being sick
and tired.

Fannie Lou Hamer

Let (racism) be a problem to someone
else. . . . Let it drag them down. Don't
use it as an excuse for your own
shortcomings.

Colin Powell

The determination to outwit one's
situation means that one has no
models, only object lessons.

James Baldwin

The Negro pays for what he wants
and begs for what he needs.

Kelly Miller

Men may not get all they pay for in
this world, but they must certainly
pay for all they get.

Frederick Douglass

If you want to keep something
secret from black folks, put it
between the covers of a book.

African-American Folk Saying

The Free in freedom
was put there
to blow your mind
to blow your game

Mari Evans

A man who will not labor to
gain his rights, is a man who would
not, if he had them, prize and
defend them.

Frederick Douglass

Has any Negro ever confessed that
civil rights can be a boring issue?
Necessary, yes, but boring as well
because it is war, and only the sick
can like war.

John A. Williams

If there is no struggle, there is no progress. Those who profess to favor freedom, and yet deprecate agitation, are men who want crops without plowing up the ground. They want rain without thunder and lightning. They want the ocean without the awful roar of its many waters. This struggle may be a moral one; or it may be a physical one; or it may be both moral and physical; but it must be a struggle. Power concedes nothing without a demand.

Frederick Douglass

Passion is not friendly. It is arrogant, superbly contemptuous of all that is not itself, and, as the very definition of passion implies the impulse to freedom, it has a mighty intimidating power. It contains a challenge. It contains an unspeakable hope.

James Baldwin

Fervor is the weapon of choice of
the impotent.

Frantz Fanon

Do not hurl a lance if you cannot
aim correctly.

The Husia

Strategy is better than strength.

Hausa Legend

Our people have made the mistake of
confusing the methods with the
objectives. As long as we agree on
objectives, we should never fall out with
each other just because we believe in
different methods or tactics or strategy. . . .
We have to keep in mind at all times
that we are not fighting for integration,
nor are we fighting for separation. We
are fighting for recognition as free
humans in this society.

Malcolm X

. . . (T)he truth is that the historical and current condition of you and yours *is* rooted in (slavery), *is* shaped by it, *is* bound to it, and *is* the reality against which all else must be gauged.

Johnnetta B. Cole

Negro action can be decisive. I say that we ourselves have the power to end the terror and to win for ourselves peace and security throughout the land.

Paul Robeson

Our nettlesome task is to discover how to organize our strength into compelling power.

Martin Luther King, Jr.

The doctrine that submission to
violence is the best cure for violence
did not hold good as between slaves
and overseers. He was whipped oftener
who was whipped easiest.

Frederick Douglass

Men who are in earnest are not
afraid of consequences.

Marcus Garvey

A man who won't die for
something is not fit to live.

Martin Luther King, Jr.

I started with this idea in my head,
"There's two things I've got a right to,
death or liberty."

Harriet Tubman

You had better all die—die immediately,
then live slaves, and entail your
wretchedness upon your posterity.
Henry Highland Garnet

Our struggle is also a struggle of
memory against forgetting.
Freedom Charter (South Africa)

When elephants fight it is the grass
that suffers.
Kikuyu Proverb

Real tragedy is never resolved.
It goes on hopelessly forever.
Chinua Achebe

. . . What you seen
Wasn't no dust of changes rising.
It was the dust of sameness settling.
Sterling Plumpp

Habit is heaven's own redress:
it takes the place of happiness.
                    Alexander Pushkin

You cannot crack a pebble,
it excludes
death . . .
It will slay
giants

but never bear children.
                    Edward Kamau Brathwaite

Voyage through death
          to life upon these shores.
                    Robert Hayden

While there's life, there's hope.
                    Terence (Publius Terentius Afer)

Identity

Moulded on Africa's anvil,
tempered down home.

Julian Bond

Africa my Africa . . .
I have never known you
But my face is full of your blood
                    David Diop

We are almost a nation of dancers,
musicians, and poets.
                    Olaudah Equiano

These people have really a great deal of
musical talent. Their songs and hymns
are so wild, so strange, and yet so
invariably harmonious and sweet. I
never listen to "Roll Jordan Roll"
without seeming to hear, almost to feel,
the rolling of waters.
                    Charlotte Forten Grimké

I, young in life, by seeming cruel
    fate
Was snatch'd from Afric's fancy'd
    happy seat.
                    Phillis Wheatley

The African, because of the violent differences between what was native and what he was forced to in slavery, developed some of the most complex and complicated ideas about the world imaginable.

Amiri Baraka

I must see (Africa), get close to it, because I can never lose the sense of being a displaced person here in America because of my color.

Paule Marshall

One ever feels his two-ness—an American, a Negro; two souls, two thoughts, two unreconciled strivings; two warring ideals in one dark body, whose dogged strength alone keeps it from being torn asunder.

W.E.B. Du Bois

For us, Afro-Christians, the naming of the
god estranged him. Ogun was an exotic
for us, not a force . . . for our invocations
were not prayer but devices. . . .
                              Derek Walcott, 1970

And I . . . keep
wandering in the mystic rhythm
of jungle drums and the concerto.
                              Gabriel Okara

No two people on earth are alike,
and it's got to be that way in music
or it isn't music.
                              Billie Holiday

I saw at a young age that apartheid was
using tribalism to deny me equal rights. . . .
                              Mark Mathabane

Had she paints, or clay, or knew the
discipline of dance, or strings; had she
anything to engage her tremendous
curiosity and her gift for metaphor, she
might have exchanged the restlessness
and preoccupation with whim for any
activity that provided her with all she
yearned for. And like any artist with no
art form, she became dangerous.

Toni Morrison

Every time I had the good fortune to
research into someone's religion I found
"God" to be the image of the people to
whom the religion belongs; that is
providing its philosophical concepts are
indigenous, not colonial.

Yosef Ben-Jochannon

They saw themselves as others had seen them. They had been formed by the images made of them by those who had had the deepest necessity to despise them.

James Baldwin

I am invisible, understand, simply because people refuse to see me.

Ralph Ellison

I felt somehow for many years that George Washington and Alexander Hamilton just left me out by mistake. But through the process of amendment, interpretation, and court decision, I have finally been included in "We, the people."

Barbara Jordan

Dependence had become a part of their second nature, and independence brought with it the cares and vexations of poverty.

Elizabeth Keckley

A climate of alienation has a profound effect on the Black personality, particularly on the educated Black, who has the opportunity to see how the rest of the world regards him and his people. It often happens that the Black intellectual thus loses confidence in his own potential and that of his race. Often the effect is so crushing that some Blacks, having evidence to the contrary, still find it hard to accept the fact we really were the first to civilize the world.

Cheikh Anta Diop

For some perverse reason, we children
hated those marigolds. . . . Perhaps we
had some dim notion of what we were,
and how little chance we had of being
anything else. Otherwise, why would
we have been so preoccupied
with destruction?

Eugenia Collier

It is a very grave matter to be forced to
imitate a people for whom you know—
which is the price of your performance
and survival—you do not exist. It is hard
to imitate a people whose existence
appears, mainly, to be made tolerable
by their bottomless gratitude that they
are not, thank heaven, *you.*

James Baldwin

History is a clock that people use to tell their time of day. It is a compass they use to find themselves on the map of human geography. It tells them where they are, and what they are.

John Henrik Clarke

Intellectuals ought to study the past not for the pleasure they find in so doing, but to derive lessons from it.

Cheikh Anta Diop

The black man who wants to turn his race white is as miserable as he who preaches hatred for the whites.

Frantz Fanon

A child born under oppression has all the elements of servility in its constitution.

Martin Delany

If you have no confidence in self you are twice defeated in the race of life. With confidence you have won even before you have started.

Marcus Garvey

Your world is as big as you make it.

Georgia Douglas Johnson

Those whom the gods would destroy they first call "promising."

Jan Carew

When you control a man's thinking you do not have to worry about his actions. You do not have to tell him not to stand here or go yonder. He will find his "proper place" and will stay in it. You do not need to send him to the back door. He will go without being told. In fact, if there is no back door, he will cut one for his special benefit.

Carter G. Woodson

He who fears is literally delivered to destruction.

Howard Thurman

I have
never been contained
except I
made
the prison

Mari Evans

Don't look back. Something may be gaining on you.

Satchel Paige

It is impossible to pretend that you are not heir to, and therefore, however inadequately or unwillingly, responsible to, and for, the time and place that give you life—without becoming, at very best, a dangerously disoriented human being.

James Baldwin

To be black is to live with anger as the defining emotion of a racial experience. To be successful is to learn how to keep the emotion from consuming or debilitating black ambition.

Audrey Edwards
Craig K. Polite

When I discover who I am, I'll be free.

Ralph Ellison

I would never be of any service to anyone as a slave.

Nat Turner

Too many black folks are fools about color and hair.

Mabel Lincoln

I am a man who perceives life in a certain way, a man who rejects things that defecate on humankind, who rejects anything that will not give people room for dissent.

Harry Belafonte

I must oppose any attempt that Negroes
may make to do to others what has
been done to them. . . . I know the
spiritual wasteland to which that road
leads . . . *whoever debases others is
debasing himself.*

James Baldwin

From adolescence to death there is
something very personal about being
a Negro in America.

J. Saunders Redding

I am not a perfect servant.
I am a public servant.

Jesse Jackson

The basic tenet of black consciousness is that the black man must reject all value systems that seek to make him a foreigner in the country of his birth and reduce his basic human dignity.
Steve Biko

Color is not a human or a personal reality; it is a political reality.
James Baldwin

The fact is that American whites, as a whole, are just as much in doubt about their nationality, their cultural identity, as are Negroes.
Harold Cruse

In America, black *is* a country.
Amiri Baraka

I am not tragically colored. There is no
great sorrow dammed up in my soul,
nor lurking behind my eyes. I do not
mind at all. . . . I do not weep at the
world—I am too busy sharpening my
oyster knife.

Zora Neale Hurston

All poor people ain't black and
all black people ain't poor.

African-American Folk Saying

Our people know that they are the
worthy repositories of human culture,
assets in the defense and perpetuity of
which so large a number of our
ancestors—forever immortal—gave their
lives; our people did not kneel to the
cultural mystification of the authorities
in occupation.

Sékou Touré

I want to be black, to know black, to
luxuriate in whatever I might be calling
blackness at any particular time, but to
do so in order to come out on the other
side, to experience a humanity that is
neither colorless nor reducible to color.
                        Henry Louis Gates, Jr.

The Negro was invented in America.
                        John Oliver Killens

I believe in pride of race and lineage
and self: in pride of self so deep as to
scorn injustice to other selves.
Especially do I believe in the Negro
Race: in the beauty of its genius, the
sweetness of its soul, and its strength in
that meekness which shall yet inherit
this turbulent earth.
                        W.E.B. Du Bois

Women

Next to God we are indebted
to women, first for life itself,
and then for making it
worth living.

Mary McLeod Bethune

We, the black women of today, must accept the full weight of a legacy wrought in blood by our mothers in chains . . . as heirs to a tradition of supreme perseverance and heroic resistance. . . .

Angela Davis

The present mincing horror at free womanhood must pass if we are ever to be rid of the bestiality of free manhood. . . .

W.E.B. Du Bois, 1920

The race cannot succeed, nor build strong citizens, until we have a race of women competent to do more than bear a brood of negative men.

T. Thomas Fortune

We are free to say that in respect to political rights, we hold women to be justly entitled to all we claim for men.

Frederick Douglass, 1848

Living in a society where the objective social position and the reputed virtues of white women smother whatever worth black women may have, the Negro male is put to judging his women by what he sees and imagines the white woman is.

Calvin Hernton, 1965

To the ordinary American or Englishman, the race question at bottom is simply a matter of ownership of women; white men want the right to use all women, colored and white, and they resent the intrusion of colored men in this domain.

W.E.B. Du Bois

I do not see how colored women can be true to themselves unless they demand recognition for themselves and those they represent.

Ida B. Wells-Barnett

That man over there says that women need to be helped into carriages, and lifted over ditches, and to have the best place everywhere. Nobody ever helps me into carriages, or over mud puddles, or gives me any best place! And ain't I a woman?

Sojourner Truth, 1851

When you're a black woman, you seldom get to do what you just want to do; you always do what you have to do.

Dorothy I. Height

Women manage, quite brilliantly, on the whole, and to stunning and unforeseeable effect, to survive and surmount being defined by others. They dismiss the definition, however dangerous or wounding it may be—or even, sometimes, find a way to utilize it—perhaps because they are not dreaming. But men are neither so supple nor so subtle. A man fights for his manhood: that's the bottom line.

James Baldwin

Only the black woman can say, "When and where I enter . . . then and there the whole race enters with me."

Anna Julia Cooper, 1892

For as unseemly as it may appear nowadays for a woman to preach, it should be remembered that nothing is impossible with God.

Jarena Lee, 1836

Black women are not here to compete or fight with you, brothers. If we have hang-ups about being male or female, we're not going to be able to use our talents to liberate all of our black people.

Shirley Chisholm

Throughout the social history of black women, children are more important than marriage in determining the woman's domestic role.

Paula Giddings

The future woman must have a life
work and economic independence.
She must have the right of motherhood
at her own discretion.

W.E.B. Du Bois, 1920

In that society (in Ghana), women
themselves believe that only two types
of their species suffer: the sterile—
that is, those incapable of producing
children—and the foolish. And by the
foolish they refer to the type of woman
who depends solely on her husband
for subsistence.

Christina Ama Ata Aidoo

There is a great stir about colored men
getting their rights but not a word about
colored women; and if colored men get
their rights and not colored women
theirs, you see, colored men will be
masters over the women.

Sojourner Truth

I had . . . found that motherhood was a
profession by itself, just like
schoolteaching and lecturing. . . .
Ida B. Wells-Barnett

Momma . . . rose alone
to apocalyptic silence,
set the sun in our windows,
and daily mended the world. . . .
Paulette Childress White

You go through so many changes as
a child, then you grow up and discover
that none of that stuff mattered,
except for the impression it made
on your mind.
Joan Walton Collaso

When in this world a man comes forward
with a thought, a deed, a vision, we ask
not how does he look, but what is his
message? . . . The world still wants to ask
that a woman primarily be pretty. . . .
W.E.B. Du Bois, 1920

In search of my mother's garden,
I found my own.

Alice Walker

When you grab hold to a woman, you
got something there. You got a whole
world there. You got a way of life kicking
up under your hand. That woman take
and make you feel like something.

August Wilson

And God said: Adam,
What hast thou done? . . .
and Adam
With his head hung down,
Blamed it on the woman.

James Weldon Johnson

All womanhood is hampered today
because the world on which it is
emerging is a world that tries to worship
both virgins and mothers and in the
end despises motherhood and
despoils virgins.

W.E.B. Du Bois, 1920

Small nations are like indecently
dressed women. They tempt the
evil-minded.

Julius Nyerere

Sisters have taught me that we should
listen to the poetry within, capture and
express our inner beauty as part of our
political and social being.

Manning Marable

But what of black women? . . . I most
sincerely doubt if any other race of
women could have brought its fineness
up through so devilish a fire.

W.E.B. Du Bois

We black women are the single group in
the West intact. And anybody can see
we're pretty shaky. We are, however (all
praises), the only group that derives its
identity from itself.

Nikki Giovanni

Perhaps she was both child and woman,
darkness and light, past and present,
life and death—all the opposites
contained and reconciled in her.
                    Paule Marshall

When we will, women won't; and when
we won't, they want to exceedingly.
                    Terence (Publius Terentius Afer)

I am a black woman
the music of my song
some sweet arpeggio of tears
is written in a minor key
and I
can be heard humming in the night
Can be heard
                    humming
in the night
                    Mari Evans

Men

I have always thanked God for
making me a man, but Martin Delany
always thanked God for making him
a black man.

Frederick Douglass

Men are not women, and a man's
balance depends on the weight he
carries between his legs.

James Baldwin

No white person knows, really knows,
how it is to grow up as a Negro boy
in the South. The taboo of the white
woman eats into the psyche, erodes
away significant portions of boyhood
sexual development, alters the total
concept of masculinity, and creates in
the Negro male a hidden ambivalence
towards all women, black as well
as white.

Calvin Hernton, 1965

I found that what the white man of
the South practiced as all right for
himself, he assumed to be unthinkable
in white women.

Ida B. Wells-Barnett, 1927

It began to seem, indeed, not entirely
frivolously, that the only thing which
prevented the South from being an
absolutely homosexual community was,
precisely, the reverberating absence
of men.

James Baldwin

That little man says women can't have
as much rights as men, 'cause Christ
wasn't a woman! Where did your Christ
come from? Where did your Christ come
from? From God and a woman! Man had
nothing to do with Him.

Sojourner Truth, 1851

A man without force is without the
essential dignity of humanity. Human
nature is so constituted, that it cannot
honor a helpless man, though it can pity
him, and even this it cannot do long if
signs of power do not arise.

Frederick Douglass, 1892

In those days men left their women for
all sorts of reasons . . . and nobody
blamed them much, because times
were hard.

Rita Dove

The harder you try to hold onto them,
the easier it is for some gal to pull
them away.

August Wilson

That marvelously mocking, salty
authority with which black men walked
was dictated by the tacit and shared
realization of the price each had paid to
be able to walk at all.

James Baldwin

I am convinced that the black man will
only reach his full potential when he
learns to draw upon the strengths and
insights of the black woman.

Manning Marable

She's just using him to keep from being by herself. That's the worst use of a man you can have.

August Wilson

His care suggested a family relationship rather than a man's laying claim.

Toni Morrison

If you are wise and seek to make your house stable, love your wife fully and righteously. . . . Kindness and consideration will influence her better than force.

The Husia

Mothers raise their daughters and let their sons grow up.

African-American Folk Saying

A man must defend himself, if only to demonstrate his fitness to defend anything else.

Frederick Douglass

Only men can develop boys into men.
Jawanza Kunjufu

A man ain't nothing but a man, but a son? Well now, that's *somebody*.
Toni Morrison

Fathers and sons arrive at that relationship only by claiming that relationship: that is by paying for it.
If the relationship of father to son could really be reduced to biology, the whole earth would blaze with the glory of fathers and sons.
James Baldwin

Bad judgment and carelessness are not punishable by rape.
Pearl Cleage

The male cannot bear very much humiliation; and he really cannot bear it, it obliterates him.
James Baldwin

We have survived the Middle Passage
and we have survived slavery. We have
survived the deadly arbitrariness of Jim
Crow and the hypocritical hatefulness of
northern discrimination. But now . . .
we face a danger more covert, more
insidious, more threatening and
potentially more *final* even than these:
the apparently sly conspiracy to do away
with Black men as a troublesome
presence in America.

William Strickland, 1989

Sooner or later all men bark.

Octavia Saint Laurent

If men could become pregnant, abortion
would be a sacrament.

Flo Kennedy

When a man keeps beating me to the
draw mentally, he begins to get
glamorous.

Zora Neale Hurston

When it comes to racism, the public school is no different from any other American institution. . . . The harrowing problems that beset Black men later in life . . . often begin in the classroom.

David J. Dent

What the (small boy) needs to know is that there are men in this world who are like him, black men, African-American men, who read and write and find the whole process of academics something valuable. . . . The epidemic of academic failure in the African-American male population is not going to stop unless we, African-American men, begin to do the job that we can do.

Spencer Holland

Young single black men can either represent a positive progressive force or one that just continues to react to crisis after crisis.

Haki R. Madhubuti

Black men must simultaneously shoulder some of the blame for their predicament and some of the responsibility for developing personal intervention strategies that will better their condition. . . . As black males, we have become partners in our demise.

Thomas A. Parham

The decisions that are made about who goes to Stanford and who goes to San Quentin are made outside the control of the black community.

Walter Allen

It is perhaps one of the great ironies of my life that so much of it has been spent trying on the one hand to get people to see me as a black man, and on the other not to write me off or apply some damnable double standard when they do.

Sylvester Monroe

Studies that bring clarity and direction
to the black male situation as an
integral part of the black
family/community are unpopular,
not easy to get published and
very dangerous.

Haki R. Madhubuti

One thing they cannot prohibit—
   The strong men . . . coming on
   The strong men gittin' stronger.
   Strong men. . . .
   Stronger. . . .

Sterling Brown, 1932

Living in America

The bright joyous dreams of freedom
to the slave faded—were sadly altered,
in the presence of that stern,
practical mother, reality.

Elizabeth Keckley, 1868

I do not believe that the meaning of the Constitution was forever "fixed" at the Philadelphia Convention. . . . To the contrary, the government they devised was defective from the start, requiring several amendments, a civil war, and momentous social transformation to attain the system of constitutional government, and its respect for the individual freedoms and human rights we hold as fundamental today.

Thurgood Marshall

America doesn't respect anything but money. . . . What our people need is a few millionaires.

Madame C. J. Walker

The Supreme Court has surrendered . . . . It has destroyed the Civil Rights Bill, and converted the Republican party into a party of money rather than a party of morals.

Frederick Douglass, 1894

Democracy, like religion, never was designed to make . . . profits less.

Zora Neale Hurston

Learning to take hold of one's life is very difficult in a culture that values property over life.

Haki R. Madhubuti

Those forces which stand against the freedom of nations are not only wrong—they are doomed to utter defeat and dishonor. . . . Colored peoples of the world are going to be free and equal no matter whose "best interests" are in the way.

Paul Robeson, 1958

The study of economic oppression
led me to realize that Negroes were
not alone but were part of an unending
struggle for human dignity the
world over.

Pauli Murray

For as long as whites enforce equality in
the price of railroad tickets, and in every
other particular, where we are required
to pay and do, and be punished, some
of us will believe that equality should be
carried to a finish.

Henry McNeal Turner, 1895

I believe in gradualism, but
90-odd years is gradual enough.

Thurgood Marshall, 1956

Madison Avenue is afraid of the dark.

Nat "King" Cole, 1957

In the South they don't care how close
you get, as long as you don't get too
high. In the North, they don't care how
high you get, as long as you don't get
too close.

African-American Folk Saying

When you are fighting for justice and
democracy; color, race, and social class
have little importance. . . . Man taken in
his totality transcends questions of race.

Jean-Bertrand Aristide

The 1990s are different from the '50s
and '60s. The new segregation of the
'90s is between the educated haves and
the uneducated have-nots.

Manning Marable

We would not underestimate the achievements of the captains of industry who . . . have produced the wealth necessary to ease and comfort; but we would give credit to the Negro who so largely supplied the demand for labor by which these things have been accomplished.

Carter G. Woodson

How unjust it is, that they who have but little should be always adding something to the wealth of the rich!

Terence (Publius Terentius Afer)

Some white people are so accustomed to operating at a competitive advantage that when the playing field is level, they feel handicapped.

Nathan McCall

There is nothing more dangerous than to build a society with a large segment of people in that society who feel that they have no stake in it; who feel that they have nothing to lose. People who have stake in their society, protect that society, but when they don't have it, they unconsciously want to destroy it.

Martin Luther King, Jr.

We have to give our children, especially black boys, something to lose. Children make foolish choices when they have nothing to lose.

Jawanza Kunjufu

Hungry men have no respect for law, authority, or human life.

Marcus Garvey

I find it hard to deplore these percentages (of blacks in the military) because they represent blacks rushing through a door that some of us opened with great work and risk.

Carl T. Rowan

This is our country. We don't have to slip around like peons or thieves in the middle of the night, asking someone for open sesame. Knock the damn door down!

Harold Washington

We don't hate nobody because of their color. We hate *oppression!*

Bobby Seale

White Americans today don't know what
in the world to do because when they
put us behind them, that's where they
made their mistake. If they had put us
in front, they wouldn't have let us look
back. But they put us behind them, and
we watched every move they made. . . .

Fannie Lou Hamer

Racism systematically verifies itself
anytime the slave can only be free
by imitating his master.

Jamil Abdullah Al-Amin (H. Rap Brown)

It has been the fashion of (Euro-)
American writers to deny that the
Egyptians were Negroes and claim that
they are of the same race as
themselves. This has, I have no doubt,
been largely due to a wish to deprive
the Negro of the moral support of
Ancient Greatness and to appropriate
the same to the white race.

Frederick Douglass, 1887

It is not so much a Negro History Week as it is History Week. We should emphasize not Negro History, but the Negro in history. What we need is not a history of selected races or nations, but the history of the world void of national bias, race hate, and religious prejudice.

Carter G. Woodson, 1926

. . . Historical facts are all pervasive and cut through the most rigid barriers of race and caste.

John Hope Franklin, 1947

History, as taught in our schools, has been a celebration of the white, male, Protestant Founding Fathers rather than the great mix of people in the American drama. . . . People who are in subordinated groups want history simply to do for them what history has already done for white males.

Mary Frances Berry, 1991

Education is the primary tool of emancipation and liberation for African-Americans in our fight for true equality in this country.

Earl G. Graves

If you can't count, they can cheat you.
If you can't read, they can beat you.

Toni Morrison

We have transformed few minds.
We have made no radical changes
in the economic servitude of
the black masses.

Adam Clayton Powell, Jr.

When poor people feel they make a difference, they vote. There's no apathy; there's disappointment.

Dorothy Tillman

When we were not paying enough attention to the needs of the poor and dysfunctional, they were physically reproducing themselves.

Lorraine Hale

The wretched of the earth do not decide to become extinct, they resolve, on the contrary, to multiply: life is their weapon against life, life is all that they have.

James Baldwin

The economic philosophy of black nationalism only means that our people need to be re-educated into the importance of controlling the economy of the community in which we live . . . which . . . means that we . . . won't have to constantly be involved in picketing and boycotting other people in other communities in order to get jobs.

Malcolm X

I have the people behind me and
the people are my strength.

Huey P. Newton

The violence complained of and
exhibited in Mississippi and other
Southern states . . . is exceptional and
peculiar. . . . It is an attack by an
aggressive, intelligent, white political
organization upon inoffensive, law-
abiding fellow citizens; a violent method
for political supremacy.

Blanche Kelso Bruce, 1876

In a racially divided society, majority
rule may become majority tyranny.

Lani Guinier

The fear that had shackled us all across
the years left us suddenly when we were
in that church, together.

Ralph David Abernathy

I know one thing we did right
Was the day we started to fight
Keep your eyes on the prize
Hold on. . . .

Civil Rights Movement Song

Too many of us are hung up on what we
don't have, can't have, or won't ever
have. We spend too much energy being
down, when we could use that same
energy—if not less of it—doing, or at
least trying to do, some of the things we
really want to do.

Terry McMillan

It . . . occurred to me that a system of
oppression draws much of its strength
from the acquiescence of its victims
who have accepted the dominant image
of themselves and are paralyzed by a
sense of helplessness.

Pauli Murray

Strength abounds in Harlem. Three hundred years of oppression and it survives. This is the task in Harlem, to see strength where it exists, to expect it to be there. . . . Even anger may show strength. It can sustain a child and protect him until he is helped to find more suitable vehicles for his ability to love and to act.

Margaret Lawrence

It is not enviable to be feared, but it is preferable to being lynched.

Ralph Wiley

Violence is as American as cherry pie.

H. Rap Brown (Jamil Abdullah Al-Amin)

Only the fool points at his origins
with his left hand.

Akan Proverb

Be not discouraged. There is a future for
you. . . . The resistance encountered
now predicates hope. . . . Only as we
rise . . . do we encounter opposition.

Frederick Douglass, 1892

Pride

If you haven't got it,
you can't show it.
If you have got it,
you can't hide it.

Zora Neale Hurston

We wish to plead our own cause. Too
long have others spoken for us. . . .
Our vices and degradation are ever
arrayed against us, but our virtues
are passed by unnoticed.

John Russwurm
Samuel Cornish, 1827

The genius of our black foremothers
and forefathers was . . . to equip black
folk with cultural armor to beat back
the demons of hopelessness,
meaninglessness, and lovelessness.

Cornel West

I will not leave South Africa, nor will I
surrender. The struggle is my life. I will
continue fighting for freedom until the
end of my days.

Nelson Mandela, 1961

Power concedes nothing without a demand. It never did and it never will. Find out just what any people will quietly submit to and you have found out the exact measure of injustice and wrong that will be imposed upon them, and these will continue till they are resisted with either words or blows or with both. The limits of tyrants are prescribed by the endurance of those whom they oppress.

Frederick Douglass, 1857

The only protection against injustice in man is power—physical, financial, and scientific.

Marcus Garvey

Let your motto be resistance! *resistance!* RESISTANCE! No oppressed people have ever secured their liberty without resistance.

Henry Highland Garnet, 1843

In Africa, there are no niggers;
and I will die before I become a nigger
for your entertainment.

Vernon Reid

I have cherished the ideal of a
democratic and free society in which all
persons live together in harmony with
equal opportunities. It is an ideal which
I hope to live for and to see realized.
But, if needs be, it is an ideal for which
I am prepared to die.

Nelson Mandela, 1964, 1990

Brothers, we have done that which we
purposed . . . we have striven to regain
the precious heritage we received from
our fathers. . . . I am resolved that it is
better to die than be a white man's
slave, and I will not complain if by dying
I save you.

Joseph Cinquez, 1839

Stop using the word "Negro." The word
is a misnomer from every point of view.
It does not represent a country or
anything else. . . . I am an African-
American. . . . I am not ashamed of my
African descent. . . . After people have
been freed, it is a cruel injustice to
call them by the same name they
bore as slaves.

Mary Church Terrell, 1949

It's not what you call us, but what
we answer to that matters.

Djuka

I would fight for my liberty so long as
my strength lasted, and if the time came
for me to go, the Lord would let them
take me.

Harriet Tubman

There was only one thing I could do—
hammer relentlessly, continually crying
aloud, even if in a wilderness, and force
open, by sheer muscle power, every
closed door.

Adam Clayton Powell, Jr.

What we see on the horizon is not the
death of black politics but its growth
and maturation.

Eddie N. Williams

We understand that politics is nothing
but war without bloodshed; and war is
nothing but politics with bloodshed.

Fred Hampton

A government which uses force to
maintain its rule teaches the oppressed
to use force to oppose it.

Nelson Mandela

. . . It doesn't mean that I advocate
violence, but at the same time I am not
against using violence in self-defense. I
don't call it violence when it's self-
defense, I call it intelligence.

Malcolm X

Violence is black children going to
school for 12 years and receiving 6
years' worth of education.

Julian Bond

The truth about injustice always
sounds outrageous.

James H. Cone

Truth-tellers are not always palatable.
There is a preference for candy bars.

Gwendolyn Brooks

Truth knows no color;
it appeals to intelligence.

Ralph Wiley

Truth is that which serves the interests
of a people. Two groups of people
locked in combat cannot be expected
to have the same truth.

Albert B. Cleage, Jr.

. . . It is time for blacks to begin the
shift from a wartime to a peacetime
identity, from fighting for opportunity
to the seizing of it.

Shelby Steele

Knowledge is the key that unlocks all
the doors. It doesn't matter what you
look like or where you come from if you
have knowledge.

Benjamin Carson

. . . We are a Black Gold Mine. And the
key that unlocks the door to these vast
riches is the knowledge of who we are—
I mean, who we *really* are.

Tony Brown

There is a "sanctity" involved with bringing a child into this world; it is better than bombing one out of it.

James Baldwin

I have always been against the death penalty. . . . I believe it is a relic of barbarism and savagery and that it is inconsistent with decent morals and the teaching of Christian ethics.

Kwame Nkrumah

. . . Violence always rebounds, always returns home.

Lerone Bennett, Jr.

The solution to poverty is not combating fertility. It's creating opportunities.

Walter Allen

Every man has a right to his own
opinion. Every race has a right to its
own action; therefore let no man
persuade you against your will,
let no other race influence you
against your own.

Marcus Garvey, 1923

We ain't what we want to be; we ain't
what we gonna be; but thank God,
we ain't what we was.

African-American Folk Saying

Self-Reliance

It is far better to be free to govern, or misgovern, yourself than to be governed by anybody else.

Kwame Nkrumah

What could be any more correct for any people than to see with their own eyes?
Molefi Kete Asante

A child who is to be successful is not reared exclusively on a bed of down.
Akan Proverb

No greater injury can be done to any youth than to let him feel that because he belongs to this or that race he will be advanced in life regardless of his own merits or efforts.
Booker T. Washington

One's work may be finished some day, but one's education never.
Alexandre Dumas, pere

For colored people to acquire learning in this country makes tyrants quake and tremble on their sandy foundation.
David Walker

The impulse to dream had been slowly
beaten out of me by experience. Now it
surged up again and I hungered for
books, new ways of looking and seeing.

Richard Wright

Education is our passport to the future,
for tomorrow belongs to the people
who prepare for it today.

Malcolm X

The so-called modern education, with all
its defects, however, does others so
much more good than it does the
Negro because it has been worked out
in conformity to the needs of those
who have enslaved and oppressed
weaker peoples.

Carter G. Woodson

Racial and denominational schools impart to the membership of their communities something which the general educational institution is wholly unable to inculcate.

Kelly Miller

It is the fool whose own tomatoes are sold to him.

Akan Proverb

At the bottom of education, at the bottom of politics, even at the bottom of religion, there must be for our race economic independence.

Booker T. Washington

We must not only be able to black boots, but to make them.

Frederick Douglass

A man's bread and butter is only insured when he works for it.

Marcus Garvey

Treat your guest as a guest for two days;
on the third day, give him a hoe!
Swahili Folk Saying

It's easy to work for somebody else;
all you have to do is show up.
Rita Warford

Actually we are slaves to the cost
of living.
Carolina Maria De Jesus

Man cannot live by profit alone.
James Baldwin

Cease to be a drudge, seek to be
an artist.
Mary McLeod Bethune

(Jazz) music has always been for me, as well as most black writers, an inspiration. . . . The ideas that emerge magically from this music often provide clarity in the work I am doing.

Paul Carter Harrison

I don't sing a song unless I feel it. The song don't tug at my heart, I pass on it. I have to believe in what I'm doing.

Ray Charles

Business? It's quite simple.
It's other people's money.

Alexandre Dumas, fils

The appearance of millionaires in any society is no proof of its affluence; they can be produced by very poor countries. . . . It is not efficiency of production which makes millionaires; it is the uneven distribution of what is produced.

Julius K. Nyerere

Somehow we are going to have to develop a concept of *enough* for those at the top and at the bottom so that the necessities of the many are not sacrificed for the luxuries of the few.

Marian Wright Edelman

He who starts behind in the great race of life must forever remain behind or run faster than the man in front.

Benjamin E. Mays

Land tenure is the key to the Gikuyu people's life; it secures for them that peaceful tillage of the soil which supplies their material needs and enables them to perform their magic and traditional ceremonies in undisturbed serenity, facing Mount Kenya.

Jomo Kenyatta *(Kamau Wa Ngengi)*

Every race and every nation should be judged by the best it has been able to produce, not by the worst.

James Weldon Johnson

No race can prosper till it learns that there is as much dignity in tilling a field as in writing a poem.

Booker T. Washington

If a man is called to be a streetsweeper, he should sweep streets even as Michelangelo painted, or Beethoven composed music, or Shakespeare wrote poetry. He should sweep streets so well that all the hosts of heaven and earth will pause to say, here lived a great streetsweeper who did his job well.

Martin Luther King, Jr.

Mastery of language affords remarkable power.

Frantz Fanon

Words spoken without meaning have no
tentacles. They float endlessly, bouncing
here and there, restless pieces of the
spirit; sent out without any mission or
specific destination, landing nowhere
and serving no purpose, except to
diminish the spirit of the speaker.

J.C. Bell

Thought is more important than art. . . .
To revere art and have no
understanding of the process that
forces it into existence, is finally not
even to understand what art is.

Amiri Baraka

Art for art's sake is just another piece
of deodorized dog-shit.

Chinua Achebe

Although the way of God is before
all people, the fool cannot find it.

The Husia

The specialism and visible success of the sciences have impressed some minds to such a degree that they have virtually identified the possibilities of human knowledge with the possibilities of science.

W.E. Abraham

Children see things very well sometimes—and idealists even better.

Lorraine Hansberry

Wisdom is not like money to be tied up and hidden.

Akan Proverb

The friend of a fool is a fool. The friend of a wise person is another wise person.

The Husia

A man must be at home somewhere
before he can feel at home everywhere.
                                    Howard Thurman

Before a group can enter the open
society, it must first close ranks.
                                    Stokely Carmichael
                                    Charles V. Hamilton

In all things that are purely social we
can be as separate as the fingers, yet
one as the hand in all things essential to
mutual progress.
                                    Booker T. Washington

Chance has never yet satisfied the hope
of a suffering people. Action, self-
reliance, the vision of self and the future
have been the only means by which the
oppressed have seen and realized the
light of their own freedom.
                                    Marcus Garvey

The political philosophy of black nationalism means that the black man should control the politics and the politicians in his own community; no more.

Malcolm X

We realize that our future lies chiefly in our own hands. We know that neither institution nor friends can make a race stand unless it has strength in its own foundation; that races, like individuals, must stand or fall by their own merit; that to fully succeed they must practice the virtues of self-reliance, self-respect, industry, perseverance, and economy.

Paul Robeson

We blacks look for leadership in men and women of such youth and inexperience, as well as poverty of education and character, that it is no wonder that we sometimes seem rudderless. . . . We see basketball players and pop singers as possible role models, when nothing could be further, in most cases, from their capacities.

Arthur Ashe

Life is a short walk. There is so little time and so much living to achieve.

John Oliver Killens

I have only just a minute,
Only sixty seconds in it,
Forced upon me—can't refuse it,
Didn't seek it, didn't choose it.
But it's up to me to use it.
I must suffer if I lose it.
Give account if I abuse it,
Just a tiny little minute—
But eternity is in it.

Benjamin E. Mays

Do not count your chickens before
they are hatched.

Aesop

We must reinforce argument
with results.

Booker T. Washington

Time is neutral and does not change
things. With courage and initiative,
leaders change things.

Jesse Jackson

Truth is proper and beautiful in all times
and in all places.

Frederick Douglass

Power in defense of freedom is greater
than power in behalf of tyranny and
oppression.

Malcolm X

Each of us has the right and the
responsibility to assess the roads which
lie ahead and . . . if the future road
looms ominous or unpromising . . . then
we need to gather our resolve and . . .
step off . . . into another direction.

Maya Angelou

The very time I thought I was lost, my
dungeon shook and my chains fell off.
                    African-American Folk Saying

We are Tilted;
but have no need to imitate the
  imitations.

We shall
    think—
    plan—
see the day whole through our assaulted
  vision,
prepare for surprises, little deaths,
  demotions,
big deaths,
all sorts of excellent frictions and hard
  hostagings.
                    Gwendolyn Brooks

If now isn't a good time for the truth I
don't see when we'll get to it.

Nikki Giovanni

Up, up, you mighty race!
You can accomplish what you will.

Marcus Garvey

Nothing succeeds like success.

Alexandre Dumas, pere

If you cain't bear no crosses,
You cain't wear no crown.

African-American Spiritual

Let a new earth rise. Let another
world be born. Let a bloody
peace be written in the sky.
Let a second generation full of
courage issue forth; let a
people loving freedom come
to growth.

Margaret Walker

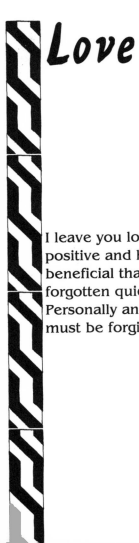

Love

I leave you love. Love builds. It is positive and helpful. It is more beneficial than hate. Injuries quickly forgotten quickly pass away. Personally and racially, our enemies must be forgiven. . . .

Mary Mcleod Bethune

Along with the idea of romantic love,
she was introduced to another—physical
beauty. Probably the most destructive
ideas in the history of human thought.
Both originated in envy, thrived in
insecurity, and ended in disillusion. In
equating physical beauty with virtue,
she stripped her mind, bound it, and
collected self-contempt by the heap.
She forgot lust and simple caring for.
She regarded love as possessive mating,
and romance as the goal of the spirit.
It would be for her a wellspring from
which she would draw the most
destructive emotions, deceiving the
lover and seeking to imprison the
beloved, curtailing freedom in
every way.

Toni Morrison

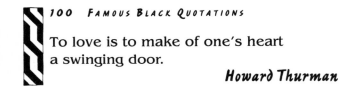

To love is to make of one's heart
a swinging door.

Howard Thurman

I have a strong suspicion . . . that much
that passes for constant love is a
golded-up moment walking in its sleep.

Zora Neale Hurston

Romance
    without finance
        don't stand a chance.

African-American Folk Saying

Being black (is) not enough. It (takes)
more than a community of skin color to
make your love come down on you.

Zora Neale Hurston

. . . Love as written about by black women will not be based on the surrender of the woman's power as it often is in the fiction of men.

Mary Helen Washington

Love is or it ain't.
Thin love ain't love at all.

Toni Morrison

Nothing that God ever made is the same thing to more than one person. That is natural. There is no single face in nature, because every eye that looks upon it, sees it from its own angle. So every man's spice-box seasons his own food.

Zora Neale Hurston

Love always sees more than is in
evidence at any moment of viewing.
Howard Thurman

Love supersedes all armies.
Dick Gregory

I refuse to accept the view that mankind
is so tragically bound to the starless
midnight of racism and war that the
bright daybreak of peace and
brotherhood can never become a
reality . . . I believe that unarmed truth
and unconditional love will have the
final word.
Martin Luther King, Jr.

They can kill all of us, but we'll continue on our peaceful route to democracy.

Limpho Hani (Mrs. Chris)

Violence as a way of achieving racial justice is both impractical and immoral. It is impractical because it is a descending spiral ending in destruction for all. . . . It is immoral because it seeks to humiliate the opponent rather than win his understanding; it seeks to annihilate rather than to convert. Violence is immoral because it thrives on hatred rather than love. . . .

Martin Luther King, Jr.

Remember, to hate, to be violent, is demeaning. It means you're afraid of the other side of the coin—to love and be loved.

James Baldwin

Not to fight at all is to choose a weapon by which one fights. Perhaps the authentic moral stature of a man is determined by his choice of weapons which he uses in his fight against the adversary. Of all weapons, love is the most deadly and devastating, and few there be who dare trust their fate in its hands.

Howard Thurman

All you need in the world is love and laughter. That's all anybody needs. To have love in one hand and laughter in the other.

August Wilson

We must turn to each other and not on each other.

Jesse Jackson

If you can't hold (children) in your arms,
please hold them in your heart.

Clara McBride Hale

The guilty furtive European notion
of sex . . . obliterates any possibility
of communion, or any hope of love.

James Baldwin

Nothing is so much to be shunned
as sex relations.

Saint Augustine

We have attempted to separate the
spiritual and the erotic, thereby
reducing the spiritual to a world of
flattened affect, a world of the ascetic
who aspires to feel nothing.

Audre Lorde

1-877- TJmX

True rebels, after all, are as rare as true
lovers, and, in both cases, to mistake a
fever for a passion can destroy one's
life.

James Baldwin

Never offer your heart
to someone who eats hearts. . . .

sail away to Africa
where holy women
await you
on the shore—
long having practiced the art
of replacing hearts
with God
and Song.

Alice Walker

One who has no sense of being
an object of love is seriously
handicapped in making someone
else an object of love.

Howard Thurman

Descendant of slave and of slave owner,
I had already been called poet, lawyer,
teacher, and friend. Now I was
empowered to minister the sacrament
of One in whom there is no north or
south, no black or white, no male or
female—only the spirit of love and
reconciliation drawing us all toward the
goal of human wholeness.

Pauli Murray

Challenge

We wanted something for ourselves
and for our children, so we took a
chance with our lives.

Unita Blackwell

Presumption should never make us
neglect that which appears easy to us,
nor despair make us lose courage at
the sight of difficulties.

Benjamin Banneker, 1794

Education remains the key to both
economic and political empowerment.

Barbara Jordan, 1991

The mere imparting of information is
not education. Above all things, the
effort must result in making a man
think and do for himself.

Carter G. Woodson, 1933

A child cannot be taught by someone
who despises him.

James Baldwin

We must nurture our children with confidence. They can't make it if they are constantly told that they won't.

George Clements

No one rises to low expectations.

Les Brown

The only justification for ever looking down on somebody is to pick them up.

Jesse Jackson

. . . People who hurt other people have usually been hurt so badly themselves that all they know how to do is hurt back.

Terry McMillan

Sexism has diminished the power of all black liberation struggles—reformist or revolutionary.

bell hooks

I never considered my race as a barrier to me. In fact, it's become an asset because it allows me to have a broader perspective.

James G. Kaiser

What you want to defeat is the idea that says your individuality doesn't count—that all you are is black. You want to say, "But I'm a person. Not a political entity."

Jamaica Kincaid

Because I want every kid to be viewed as a person rather than as a member of a certain race does not mean that I'm not black enough. . . . Do they want me to be positive just for black kids and negative for everybody else?

Michael Jordan

The mind does not take its complexion
from the skin. . . .

Frederick Douglass, 1849

Blackness is not a hairstyle. It is not a
dashiki. Judge my blackness by the jobs
that we have, by the money we are able
to generate in the community. . . .

Bertha Knox Gilkey

Why pose and posture a self that is
other than you, when I know your true
name.

Leon Forrest

Dissension is healthy, even when
it gets loud.

Jennifer Lawson

It ain't nothing to find no starting place
in the world. You just start from where
you find yourself.

August Wilson

It is critical that we take charge of our
own destiny and stop waiting for some
unknown mythical being to come along
and wipe racism from the face of
this earth.

David C. Wilson

I thought I could change the world.
It took me a hundred years to figure out
I can't change the world. I can only
change Bessie. And honey, that ain't
easy either.

Bessie Delany

Can't nothin make your life work if you ain't the architect.

Terry McMillan

The only protection against genocide is to remain necessary.

Jesse Jackson

A people who are truly strong should be able to look soberly at both their accomplishments and their problems— past and present.

Michael Blakey

Knowledge of one's identity, one's self, community, nation, religion, and God, is the true meaning of resurrection, while ignorance of it signifies hell.

Elijah Muhammad

It's better to be prepared for an opportunity and not have one than to have an opportunity and not be prepared.

Whitney Young

I had to make my own living and my own opportunity. . . . Don't sit down and wait for the opportunities to come; you have to get up and make them.

Madame C.J. Walker, 1914

Opportunity follows struggle. It follows effort. It follows hard work. It doesn't come before.

Shelby Steele, 1991

When you are looking for obstacles, you can't find opportunities.

J.C. Bell

The individual who can do something
that the world wants done will,
in the end, make his way regardless
of his race.

Booker T. Washington, 1901

It would be against all nature for all the
Negroes to be either at the bottom, top,
or in between. . . . We will go where the
internal drive carries us like everybody
else. It is up to the individual.

Zora Neale Hurston, 1942

Our elevation must be the result of
self-efforts and work of our own hands.
No other human power can accomplish
it. If we but determine it shall be so,
it will be so.

Martin R. Delany, 1852

I have discovered in life that there are ways of getting almost anywhere you want to go, if you really want to go.

Langston Hughes

A person without faith has no future.

Michael J. Cheatham

. The tragedy in life doesn't lie in not reaching your goal. The tragedy lies in having no goal to reach. It isn't a calamity to die with dreams unfulfilled, but it is certainly a calamity not to dream. It is not a disaster to be unable to capture your ideal, but it is a disaster to have no ideal to capture.

Benjamin E. Mays

If you run, you might lose. If you don't run, you're guaranteed to lose.

Jesse Jackson

Fortune favors the bold.

Terence *(Publius Terentius Afer)*

How can a man live out the length of his fiery days without a vision-prize?

Leon Forrest

If you don't dream, you might as well be dead.

George Foreman

When life knocks you down, try to fall on your back because if you can look up, you can get up.

Les Brown

In every crisis there is a message. Crises are nature's way of forcing change— breaking down old structures, shaking loose negative habits so that something new and better can take their place.

Susan L. Taylor

I believe . . . that living on the edge,
living in and through your fear, is the
summit of life, and that people who
refuse to take that dare condemn
themselves to a life of living death.

John H. Johnson

I don't know the key to success, but
the key to failure is trying to
please everybody.

Bill Cosby

The thing that makes you exceptional, if
you are at all, is inevitably that which
must also make you lonely.

Lorraine Hansberry

Where is the power? Not on the outside,
but within. . . . Thoughts are things.
You are the thinker that thinks the
thought, that makes the thing. If you
don't like it, then change your thoughts.
Make it what you want it to be.

Johnnie Colemon

You have to know that your real home
is within.

Quincy Jones

. . . Out of the heart are the issues of
life and no external force, however great
and overwhelming, can at long last
destroy a people if it does not first win
the victory of the spirit against them.

Howard Thurman

If I didn't define myself for myself,
I would be crunched into other people's
fantasies for me and eaten alive.

Audre Lorde

Whatever we believe about ourselves
and our ability comes true for us.

Susan L. Taylor

Making Discoveries

We get closer to God as we get more intimately and understandingly acquainted with the things He has created. I know of nothing more inspiring than that of making discoveries for one's self.

George Washington Carver

There is something in every one of you
that waits and listens for the sound of
the genuine in yourself. It is the only
true guide you will ever have. And if you
cannot hear it, you will all of your life
spend your days on the ends of strings
that somebody else pulls.

Howard Thurman

This feeling of being loved and
supported by the Universe in general
and by certain recognizable spirits in
particular is bliss.

Alice Walker

There are roads out of the secret places
within us along which we all must move
as we go to touch others.

Romare Bearden

With writing, you hear voices and give
yourself over to them and they become
flesh and blood by putting pen to paper.
With acting, the voices become flesh
and blood through the instrument of
your body. Either way, it's mysticism
that I'm interested in.

Regina Taylor

I write from my knowledge not my lack,
from my strength not my weakness. I
am not interested if anyone knows
whether or not I am familiar with big
words, I am interested in trying to
render big ideas in a simple way. I am
interested in being understood not
admired. I wish to celebrate and not be
celebrated. . . .

Lucille Clifton

In my writing, as much as I could,
I tried to find the good, and praise it.
Alex Haley

When I write, I write reaching . . . for
what will nod Black heads over common
denominators. . . . If there are those
outside the Black experience who hear
the music and can catch the beat, that
is serendipity; I have no objections. But
when I write, I write . . . for my people.
Mari Evans

There's no idea in the world that is not
contained by black life. I could write
forever about the black experience
in America.

August Wilson

What could I dream of that had the barest possibility of coming true? I could think of nothing. And, slowly, it was upon exactly that nothingness that my mind began to dwell, that constant sense of wanting without having, of being hated without reason.

Richard Wright

Any writer, I suppose, feels that the world into which he was born is nothing less than a conspiracy against the cultivation of his talent—which attitude certainly has a great deal to support it.

James Baldwin

I think it's hard to make a living as a writer, but I think it's hard to work at McDonald's too. . . . I think the commitment is to get up everyday and say, "I'm a writer, therefore what I'm supposed to do today is write." And to do that, and to do that and to do that.

Pearl Cleage

An artist must be free to choose what he does, certainly, but he must also never be afraid to do what he might choose. . . . We younger Negro artists who create now intend to express our individual dark-skinned selves without fear or shame. . . . We build our temples for tomorrow, strong as we know how, and we stand on top of the mountain, free within ourselves.

Langston Hughes, 1926

When you're creating your own shit . . . even the sky ain't the limit.

Miles Davis

We see things not as they are, *but as we are.* Our perception is shaped by our previous experiences.

Dennis Kimbro

Pictures just come to my mind and
I tell my heart to go ahead.

Horace Pippin

(My parents) were comfortable with me
exploring areas that they were not
proficient in. Some parents just aren't
comfortable with that.

Mae Jemison

I took up with the Beats because that's
what I saw taking off and flying and
somewhat resembling myself. The open
and implied rebellion—of form and
content. Aesthetic as well as social and
political. But I saw most of it as Art. . . .

Amiri Baraka

I had to do what I was doing if I was going to keep thinking of myself as a *creative* artist.

Miles Davis

I am not a blues singer. I am not a jazz singer. I am not a country singer. But I am a singer who can sing the blues, who can sing jazz, who can sing country.

Ray Charles

The Igbo world is an arena for the interplay of forces. It is a dynamic world of movement and of flux. Igbo art, reflecting this world view is never tranquil, but mobile and active, even aggressive.

Chinua Achebe

The black encounter with the absurd in
racist American society yields a
profound spiritual need for human
affirmation and recognition. Hence,
the centrality of religion and music—
those most spiritual of human
activities—in black life.

Cornel West

I cannot fight prejudice (in America)
and paint at the same time!

Henry Ossawa Tanner

The Blues has been the foundation
for all other American music since
the beginning.

Willie Dixon

That's our role to add artistry to
American culture.

Ralph Ellison

Waiting is a window opening on many landscapes. . . . To continue one's journey in the darkness with one's footsteps guided by the illumination of remembered radiance is to know courage of a peculiar kind—the courage to demand that light continue to be light even in the surrounding darkness. To walk in the light while darkness invades, envelops, and surrounds is to wait on the Lord. This is to know the renewal of strength. This is to walk and faint not.

Howard Thurman

I do not need to go looking for "happenings," the absurd, or the surreal because I have seen things that neither Dali, Beckett, Ionesco, nor any of the others could have thought possible; and to see these things I did not need to do more than look out of my studio window.

Romare Bearden

The fact is, nothing great or enduring in music has ever sprung full-fledged from the brain of any master; the best he gives the world he gathers from the hearts of the people, and runs it through the alembic of his genius.

James Weldon Johnson

I was born with music within me.

Ray Charles

People ask where [the stories] come from—I don't know and I'm not bothering it, because if I keep bothering it I am not going to be able to do it.

J. California Cooper

I've always told the musicians in my band to play what they *know* and then play *above that*. Because then anything can happen, and that's where great art and music happens.

Miles Davis

Since new developments are the products of a creative mind, we must therefore stimulate and encourage that type of mind in every way possible.

George Washington Carver

No amount of persuasion can change a man's reaction to what he knows.
But what he knows can be changed, and the most direct manner is to alter the images within his mind.

Dennis Kimbro

Film is not to be played with. It may be our most powerful medium and should be treated as such.

Spike Lee

Real education means to inspire people to live more abundantly, to learn to begin with life as they find it and make it better. . . .

Carter G. Woodson

Negro dialect poetry had its origin in the minstrel traditions . . . (and) the writers wrote chiefly to entertain an outside audience, and in concord with its stereotyped ideas about the Negro. And herein lies the vital distinction between them and the folk creators who wrote solely to please and express themselves.

James Weldon Johnson, 1931

The profitable literary scam nowadays is to pose as someone who airs unpleasant and frank facts about the black community, only to be condemned by the black community for doing so. This is the sure way to grants, awards, prizes, fellowships, and academic power.

Ishmael Reed, 1994

I believe that all literatures can have political uses and misuses. Sometimes politics can enhance, sometimes it can get in the way of imaginative literature. . . . I'm not sure one can be a creative writer and a politician—not a "good" politician.

Gayl Jones

I did not believe political directives could be successfully applied to creative writing . . . not to poetry or fiction, which to be valid had to express as truthfully as possible the individual emotions and reactions of the writer.

Langston Hughes

There must be possible a fiction which, leaving sociology and case histories to the scientists, can arrive at the truth about the human condition, here and now, with all the bright magic of the fairy tale.

Ralph Ellison

The best art is political and you ought to
be able to make it unquestionably
political and irrevocably beautiful at the
same time.

Toni Morrison

It's not a ladder we're climbing, it's
literature we're producing. . . .
We cannot possibly leave it to history
as a discipline nor to sociology nor
science nor economics to tell the
story of our people.

Nikki Giovanni

The colonized man who writes for his
people ought to use the past with the
intention of opening the future, as an
invitation to action and a basis for hope.

Frantz Fanon

Rappers are fearless. We have the power to generate thoughts, make people second guess the system. So, of course, I become an enemy of the system when I talk about the system. . . . And maybe that's what really scares people about rap—not that it has the power to stir up trouble, but that it makes us think about troubles we'd just as soon shove under the table.

Ice Cube

We cannot silence the voices that we do not like hearing. We can, however, do everything in our power to make certain that other voices are heard.

Deborah Prothrow-Stith

Poetry is a *subconscious conversation,* it is as much the work of those who understand it as those who make it.

Sonia Sanchez

The white fathers told us, "I think, therefore, I am" and the black mother within each of us—the poet—whispers in our dreams, I feel, therefore I can be free. Poetry coins the language to express and charter this revolutionary demand.

Audre Lorde

The job of the writer is to make revolution irresistible.

Toni Cade Bambara

My aim, in my next future, is to write poems that will somehow successfully "call" all black people. . . . Not always to "teach"—I shall wish often to entertain, to illumine.

Gwendolyn Brooks

Art, no matter what its intention, reacts to or reflects the culture it springs from.

Sonia Sanchez

This is the time when your life
  is revealed
Everything is possible,
  but nothing is real.

Vernon Reid

The understanding of art depends
finally upon one's willingness to
extend one's humanity and one's
knowledge of human life.

Ralph Ellison

INDEX

Friday

God's spirit is a constant source of joy that gladdens my soul.

Joy

Joy shines out from the window of my soul as gladness that enriches my thoughts and conversations, my perceptions and experiences. I give thanks to God for being my ever-present source of joy.

"Dear God, my gratitude for You increases every day. Your spirit within me is a constant source of joy that gladdens my soul. Joy shines out from me to reveal Your presence all around me. I know Your spirit is within me and surrounding me at all times.

"Thank You, God, for the joy I feel in quiet moments spent being aware of You and only You. I feel Your presence expressed in the joy of my loved ones and friends.

"Thank You, God, for joy—a rejoicing of being in Your presence."

> "You bestow on him blessings forever;
> you make him glad with the joy of
> your presence."
>
> —Psalm 21:6

Saturday

Wherever I am, I am at home with God.

Moving

Moving out of a home I have been in for many years or even just a few years can be a traumatic experience. I may feel as if I am leaving a major part of my life behind as I move away from familiar spaces, friends, and neighborhoods.

Yet what helps me make the move with peace of mind is that I realize all that I am taking with me. I have cherished memories of people and times that hold a special place in my heart. There is much I have to offer in the way of friendship to new people I meet in new places.

Most important, the presence of God goes with me to my new home, neighborhood, or job. This new beginning is one in which I am at home with God wherever I may be.

"For the cloud of the Lord was on the tabernacle by day, and fire was in the cloud by night, before the eyes of all the house of Israel at each stage of their journey."—Exodus 40:38

ABOUT THE EDITOR

Janet Cheatham Bell's parents brought home hard-to-come-by books by African-American writers during her childhood in Indianapolis, thus igniting for her a lifetime study of the history and culture of African-Americans.

She has taught African-American literature at a number of colleges and universities, and been associate editor of *The Black Scholar*. In 1972, with St. Clair Drake and Ronald W. Bailey at Stanford University, she authored the curriculum review, *Teaching Black*. Until 1984 she was a senior editor of literature textbooks with a major educational publisher.

Ms. Bell currently lives in Chicago where she is a freelance writer and editor.

abrogation

I like Samson using the Jawbone of an ass.